You're the Best Parent for Your Child: 31 Truths from AskMoxie.org

Magda Pecsenye

ISBN: 0692344926
ISBN-13: 978-0692344927

Dedication

To all the parents trying to do the best they can for their kids.

Contents

Acknowledgments

Thank you to Kristina ElSayed for sensitive and insightful comments on the manuscript and for understanding what it's about.

Thank you to Gene Butcher for the perfect cover photo and for steadfast support.

Thank you to all the readers of AskMoxie.org for the past nine years, and to everyone in the Ask Moxie Facebook group, for your support and comments and good humor.

Introduction

August is the cruelest month, at least on the internet. For some reason, everyone seems to get extremely cranky on the internet during the month of August. People get into fights, and block people, and forward all sorts of passive-aggressive quote graphics, and just generally get upset about small things and major things. It's exhausting, and it's way too easy to get sucked in.

This year I thought I'd try to head the August Anger off at the pass by posting on AskMoxie.org every day with something that I'd learned was true in all my years of parenting. Not aphorisms, really, but truths that grew with you as your kid grew, and as your relationship with your kid deepened and changed.

The first few days were easy. And then it started to get a little more real. And by the end I was feeling for all of us about how much work this actually all is, and how deeply we love and need our kids, and how changed we are.

I hope that you find some truth in my truths.

You are the best parent for your child.

Courage.

Magda Pecsenye

December 2014

1: You can do it

You can do it.

Yes, this should maybe be the finale of the month of parenting truths, but it's really the most important of all the true things about parenting. You can do it. Even when things get really tough. Even when you're so exhausted and wish you hadn't had your kids, or wish you could just hand them to someone else to be responsible for for a few days, or want to run away completely. Even when you're doing really well and are the parent you want to be and are worried that things are going to fall apart any minute. Even when you think you're going to break.

You can do it.

And you will do it. You'll keep waking up, and showing up, and being there for your kids. Even when you're not making all the right choices and being as focused and shiny as you want to be. Even when you think everything you touch turns to utter shit. Even when you're singing a lullaby with your mouth but your brain is somewhere else, back when you were still the old you.

You will do it.

When your baby is six months, and three years, and nine years, and sixteen years. You will do it as the challenges change and become more high-stakes. You will do it as your children start to leave you while they still need you. You will do it forever, because you are you, and you are love.

2: Parenting taps into a lot of anger

This one can be hard to process, especially if you were raised not to acknowledge or express anger. Parenting can tap into a lot of anger, even serious rage, at all kinds of people and situations. It's a combination of the parenting hormones (which parents develop from contact with their kids, so parents who didn't give birth to their kids also develop these hormones) and the intensity of the love and stress of caring for kids. Suddenly you see things with new eyes, and you're more attuned to vulnerability and injustice, to power imbalances and to cruelty of all sorts. All that can tap into anger you never knew you had (or had already worked to balance or overcome).

It can be scary, this anger. You may not feel anger at your actual child until they're older than baby age (or maybe you do--that's ok, too), but the feeling of rage at the injustices in the world and how little control you have over things can wash over you when you least expect it and feel least equipped to deal with it. It comes in waves, and tends to crest whenever your child is entering a new phase that requires new skills or focus from you. And then once you get your feet under you again it'll subside.

It's all normal and ok, unless the anger feels like it's taking over your emotions completely and preventing you from engaging or enjoying things. If the anger feels like it's bigger than it should be, talk to someone. This is a symptom of hormonal imbalance or post-partum depression (men and mothers who didn't give birth also get post-partum depression), and you need to work your way through it with someone who knows how to help you deal with it and get it back to its proper, manageable mass in your life.

(Don't forget Day 1: You can do it. You can do it and you are doing it.)

3: It's still early in the game

Unless your kids are over 40, it's still really early in your parenting career. And a lot is going to change.

It can feel pretty bleak when you're going through sleepless nights with a baby, or the willfulness of a two-year-old, or any minute of every day of having a 3.5-year-old. And you may be wondering if it's ever going to get better. But those kids are still so little, and it's all going to change. They're still so small in the scope of things. Even when your kids are 7, or 12, or 16, it still all changes all the time.

You are having a long conversation with your child, and it's going to last the rest of your lives. This tough part at the beginning feels so high stakes, like everything that happens is so important, but it's actually such a small little preliminary chat in comparison to the deep emotional discussions you'll have later.

Pace yourself. There's a lot more (and a lot more fun) still to come. It changes, and gets easier, and then harder, and then easier, and then harder. But it always changes. You'll learn as you go, so you're ready for it when it happens, as it gets more challenging.

You are doing it.

4: You are not SuperMom (or SuperDad)

There's a whole culture of calling parents who are doing a lot of things "SuperMom!!" or "SuperDad!!" that is meant to praise, but is instead really constricting.

Because it assumes that we a) want to be doing all this stuff, and b) should be doing all this stuff, and c) aren't being negatively affect by all this stress. It assumes that busier is better. That doing it alone with no help is somehow honorable. That "making it look easy" is praise-worthy.

But the truth is that we're tired and stressed and sometimes lonely. We're doing too much, because we have to. And sometimes because in order to do the things that we love, we have to add them on to all the stuff that just has to get done. And it doesn't mean there's anything particularly valiant or morally superior or even extra-strength about us. It just means we're making it, one day at a time.

If you are making it, one day at a time, good for you. If you're making it look easy because you don't express stress externally, that's great. If you're making it because you ask for help, that's great. If you're making it because you complain through it, that's great. Whatever gets you through the crucible of being a parent along with everything else you have to do. Try to give yourself breaks, and don't worry about making sure all your self-care is organic and hand-picked and healthy. Sometimes you just want to sit alone in your car and listen to *The Low-End Theory* all the way through while eating Red Vines. And that's ok.

You are a person. Who has kids and a bunch of other stuff to take care of. And sometimes you keep all the balls in the air and sometimes you don't. But you're still you, and you're still worthy, even if you don't have a cape or a smile on your face.

Keep going.

5: You will fail

There's that quote "What would you do if you knew you could not fail?" But that makes no sense to me. No one who tries anything is fail-proof. I'd rather ask, "What would you do if you knew you'd fail repeatedly but that failure would lead to success you can't even imagine now?"

Would you try? Of course you would. Because the results are worth it, even if the shame and guilt of failure stings in the moment. This is life. And this is parenting.

You are going to fail. You'll fail yourself whenever you aren't the parent you want to be or think you should be. You'll fail in your non-parent life and duties because sometimes life is too overwhelming and you have too much on your plate. And you'll fail your kids sometimes, too.

That's the one that stings the most. When you fail your kids. The first time your child is in your arms you look at that sweet face and vow never to do anything that will hurt them. But part of being human is being flawed. Making mistakes. Sometimes making mistakes that really hurt someone. But hurting your child doesn't mean everything's broken. It means you learn to repair things. It means you take the rubbed spots and that's where you grow closer. Stronger at the scars.

The only way to avoid failing as a parent is not to be a parent. And you're a parent, so you'll fail sometimes. Be gentle with yourself, then rub some dirt on it and hug your kid and get back in there. You're worth it, and so are your kids.

Courage.

6: Your kid is going to be the same person forever

In those early days, when your baby is slowly waking up from being inside the womb for so long and learning to interface with the outside world, you pay attention so carefully. You watch how your child moves, how your child approaches the world and taking in information, and how your child interacts with other people.

Flash forward ten years and your child moves and takes in info and interacts the same way.

Flash forward another ten years, another thirty years, and it's the same thing.

Parenting your child is about knowing what to facilitate and what to scaffold, what to help manage and what to encourage. But your child is going to be the same essential person forever. That means that as you grow together you get to know and understand each other more and more, and learn what makes each of you bloom.

It's a big chance to learn to love each other the way you each need to be loved. As the parent, you get to guide that. And it starts by watching carefully, and being open to who this wonderful little person is. And then helping them become even more of that as they grow in skills and ability to communicate.

It's a wonderful life, this chance to love someone for decades, and to watch how they unfold.

7: This is a long conversation

I've written about this before: Parenting is a loooooong conversation with your kid. I touched on it yesterday, that you get years and years to watch your child's personality unfold. But you also get all those years to communicate with each other and learn each other.

Everything you do is part of the conversation. Every hug. Every fight. Every time you help your child learn a new skill. Every time you scold your child for not doing something. Every time you discipline your child or teach your child or praise your child. Every heart-to-heart you have. Every time they ask you about sex and you answer (or, unfortunately, don't answer). Every time you tell them something they should know, or show them who you are by what you do. It's all part of this epic conversation that lasts for as many decades as you're lucky enough to have together.

That means that no one single interaction is going to ruin things. Even a long stretch of bad interactions won't ruin things. As long as you can keep the conversation as loving and supportive as it can be, occasional bad interactions won't knock things off the track.

Play the long game. Decide what you want the conversation to feel like, for you and for your child. And then keep returning to that whenever you can, even when an interaction goes poorly.

Courage.

8: Parenting hurts (emotionally)

Ouch. Nothing breaks your heart like feeling rejected by your child. (Unless it's feeling like you failed your child.) Whether it's as simple as your baby refusing to nurse, or your toddler pushing away food you've made, or your preschooler saying "I hate you!" The 3.5-year horribleness or the 9-year-old tantrums. The eye rolling or the not wanting to be kissed in public anymore.

But as I said yesterday, remember that this is a long, looooooong conversation you have with your child. Not everything is going to be good. Some of it is going to be bad. Some of it will hurt your heart. But as the parent, you owe it to yourself not to get too hurt. Instead of thinking it's about you, listen to the feeling behind your child's behavior, and see if you can help your kid get through whatever it is. Refusing to nurse? Could be teething pain, a nursing strike, overtiredness. You can help. Pushing away food? Greater need for independence, so you can start giving two limited choices so your kid feels empowered. Saying "I hate you"? What is your child feeling pushed by that's making them feel so powerless and defensive? You can help.

Yes, it hurts, but the rejection of your child is just the symptom. If you can stay quiet and listen even more closely, you can figure out how to help your child manage their feelings and the situation better. And then you'll be able to move on to a better part of the long conversation.

You're doing this.

9: Parenting hurts (physically)

This is something no one tells you: Being a parent is like doing CrossFit with a really strong, risk-taking, ill-tempered-but-adorable monkey trainer. You will sustain physical injuries.

Let's not even talk about pregnancy and delivery, because that's too horrifying and it's basically one long injury. Let's talk about tennis elbow and tendinitis from carrying the baby. Back problems from hunching over while feeding the baby. Concussions from toddlers and preschoolers. Chronic sleep problems. Jaw pain from clenching while you worry about your child in school.

This is no joke. It's painful, and it's hurtful, too. Physical pain hurts your feelings. And most of this pain happens long before your child is old enough to understand and be careful of you physically.

There will be a day, however, when your child begins to understand that they can take as much care with you as you take with them. When your child starts protecting you and your body as much as you protect your child. It takes years, and a lot of stress on your body, to get to that part of the conversation. But you'll get there.

In the meantime, lift with your legs.

10: Your kid is going to think about things you don't know anything about

I remember when my older son was a baby and I couldn't wait to find out what he was thinking about. And then he started talking, and I knew what he was thinking during every waking moment. It was strange, this intimate knowledge of someone else's inner life, but I loved it. And then suddenly he started talking about things I knew nothing about, and I realized he had a life that didn't involve me in every moment anymore.

It happens with every child. Eventually they develop an interest in something you know nothing about, and you suddenly know that at some point that child will have a whole big wide life that isn't anchored to you.

Maybe it's dinosaurs. Or Greek myths. With my son it was baseball statistics. He was five years old, and he became obsessed with baseball and baseballs stats. I don't like baseball and I have no interest in baseball stats, so I wasn't even tempted to try to cram to catch up to him. I just let him tell me what he knew, and feigned interest so he knew I always wanted to hear what he had to say. And you'll listen and marvel at where your child's interests lie, too, and let them talk and talk and talk (even when you really don't care about the content of what they're saying).

One of my friends attended her son's PhD dissertation defense last week. Someday this will be you. Or maybe it won't be a dissertation defense, but it'll be a promotion at work, or some sort of award, or even just listening to your kid explain something they're really good at to someone else. You'll be just as proud then as you are the first time, and a lot less surprised.

It's good when you get to the part of the conversation in which your child is teaching you new things. Keep going.

11: No one comes out unscathed

No matter what you do, you aren't going to parent your children perfectly. And even if you could be the perfect parent, there are too many other things that happen to people in their first 18 years that hurt them. No one comes out of childhood unscathed.

Everyone could go to therapy. A lot of us roll along, functioning decently. But we'd probably all be better off if we spent six months seeing a good therapist who could help us identify and come to terms with the stuff that happened when we were kids, and then help us make a plan to act in ways that lead us to connection and fulfillment instead of re-enacting old hurts and patterns. To change how we think and act so we can have better relationships and feel more satisfied.

This is just life. No matter how many things you do correctly.

No matter how many good decisions you make. No matter how attentive or correct or research-backed or selfless or good-enough you are. Because your kids are of this world, so they're going to be hurt somehow at some point. You can't possibly protect them from everything.

You can feel despair about it, or you can realize that this releases you from having to be perfect and instead allows you to be better. Knowing that SOMETHING is going to hurt your kids, you get to minimize the big things that are in your control. You get to pick what you protect them from and what you let them experience. What they learn to handle early and what you scaffold them in for longer. Being mindful of their individual personalities, and of your own resources.

And you know that there are some things that you can't control. All you can do is be there to help your kids through them, so they don't have to process alone. Helping them process gives them skills they wouldn't develop--skills they'll need for later on--that they couldn't develop if you protected them from everything.

Then, when your kids are adults, and they start working through the stuff that happened when they were kids, stay close. You know you did the best you could, so you don't have to justify yourself. Listen with open ears and an open heart. Be willing to analyze and debrief when your kids need to.

Apologize if things got past you that hurt them. Know that as your kids come to terms with things you can stay close if you stay open.

Life is hard. But we have each other.

12: You'll have to talk about hard things

I have depression. So I've talked to my kids about depression for years, so they know what it is, and that they have a risk for it, and how it may or may not affect them.

It's only one of the hard things we've talked about--divorce is another one that we live every day, and we lived through my grandmother's slow death from Alzheimer's, and they know what happened on 9/11--so they're used to my sitting them down and telling them we need to talk about something that I trust them enough to understand.

Other families have hard things that they live with, too, everything from illness to discrimination to death to job loss, and more. There's a lot of trouble in the world, and kids don't get a pass to escape it.

Because there's sadness in the world, you are going to have

to have some hard conversations with your kids. You'll probably talk to them about depression and divorce, even if those don't touch your family as intimately as they touch mine, along with all the other tough things that they live through or observe. You'll talk to them about all sorts of things that happen that we wish we didn't have to confront. The only way for them to learn about the world is either to hear it from you or to live it. And I'm guessing you'd rather have their introduction to the bad things be with you so you can help them through it. If you talk to them about the tough things you get the chance to help your kids make sense of it all, and to be able to cope. So don't be afraid of the tough conversations, because that's where you build trust.

You can do it.

13: The past is your ally

All of us had childhoods. Those of us who were lucky want to replicate a lot of what the people who took care of us did, or build on it. Others who weren't so lucky want to do everything differently. Most people want to do something in between what happened to us and the opposite of what happened to us.

This means that the past is our biggest help, because it's our biggest teacher. You know what happens when you treat a child the way you were treated under the conditions you were raised in--you're the outcome of that treatment. (If you have any siblings who were treated the same way, they're the outcome of that treatment, too.) If you account for the differences between your childhood situation and your children's situation, you can predict what will happen to your children if you treat them the same way you were treated. And you can adjust your parenting from that to get the results that you want to get.

The past can hurt and be hard to confront. But it's the best information you have about how children grow and develop, so it's worth putting in the time and analysis and friction to consider carefully how you were raised and how that affected you.

You can choose any future you want. But only if you look at the past with clear eyes and learn the lessons it teaches you. You and your kids are worth it.

Keep going.

14: You owe your kid the truth

Your child deserves to know the truth about the world. About people, about racism and discrimination, about how we have to be conscious of our own behavior in the world. And you're the best person to teach them the truth.

You don't have to sit them down to have A Talk, because there are things happening all the time that you can use to teach your child. Every day gives you chances to observe the injustices in the world, the wrong information, and the logical consequences, and explain that to your kid. There have been some extremely difficult tragic events lately, including the killings of Mike Brown and Eric Garner, and the protests in response to those killings. You need to talk to your child when these things happen, to explain what happened, why it happened, and what we can do in response.

Depending on how old your child is, you may not be able to talk to them in depth yet, and some things may be too scary for them. But if you start getting in the habit of observing the world around you and talking about it, by the time they are old enough to learn about prejudice and racism and discrimination, they'll be used to talking openly and knowing their questions will be answered. You won't have to be afraid that you won't be able to say the right things, because you'll know you have a lot of chances to get your message across.

It's really REALLY important for kids to know what their world is about. Even when that's unpleasant. If you tell them, you can help them think about it and fit it into their developing view of the world. If you let them hear about it somewhere else, they have no help from you to process it.

So please, talk to your kids about racism, privilege, institutionalized bias of all types, and the fact that we can all stop it, but only by exposing it whenever we encounter it.

15: The better a parent you are the less they need you

This one hits me hard every few months: The better a job I do at teaching my kids to love and trust themselves and find home within themselves, the less they'll need me eventually. The measure of my success will be that they don't need me to lead them or buffer things for them anymore. Whether they go away geographically or not, they'll take the reins of their own lives.

Kids need to grow out of needing their parents. As much as we want to keep doing things for them, keep helping them with their emotions, keep owning the sweet smells of their heads and their gorgeous peals of laughter, it's not healthy to hold on so tightly. We scaffold and support and nurture and teach, until our children can do everything they need to do to be functioning members of society. Without us.

So the better we are at parenting, the more able they'll be to fly away from us.

The good news is that the better a parent any of us is the more they'll want to be around us later. Eventually. Once they're done doing everything they want to do. And if they have kids of their own. Wanting to be near us is better than needing to be near us, because it implies choice, and deep love, and interdependence instead of dependence.

Keep going. Keep doing it right.

16: It hurts you more when they leave than it hurts them

Expanding on what I said about knowing that it's good when they don't need you anymore, another truth is that it hurts you more when they leave than it hurts them.

When your children leave you it's to go to a fun babysitter, or preschool, or summer camp, or college. Someplace fun and new with things to do and learn and new friends to make and wings to stretch out and theories to test. In the meantime, you're stuck at home alone or on a plane somewhere or at your desk at work. And it's not that thrilling and you wonder how your child is doing and you miss their sweet little head.

Yes, there are times when you're dying to get away from them for a bit, when you're jumping out of your own skin from being touched or want to rip your ears out rather than hear "Whyyyyyyy???" one more time. And there are times when your kids really, really, REALLY want to be with you. But for the most part, your kids are more excited about leaving you than you are about their leaving. And when they're gone you feel more of a hole than they do.

That's good. It means you've given them enough to have confidence in themselves and to feel secure without you. So while it can sting a little that they don't feel as homesick for you as you do for them, it's all part of creating wonderful people who can go into the world with confidence.

You're doing it.

17: You can ask for help

Parents aren't meant to do this alone. Children are a common good, for one thing, so it benefits everyone to help parents raise children. And this whole nuclear-family-one-or-two-adults-alone-in-a-house-with-children-24/7 thing is extremely new historically and totally maladaptive, in my opinion.

So ask for help when you need it. Ask for help before you need it.

You may be emotionally hurt by parenting, or lonely, or just done. That's all normal. A chat with a friend or relative who loves you and will let you vent without telling you to be grateful can be just the thing to give you the strength to get through bedtime. Reach out when you need validation, commiseration, or just someone to tell you they like you.

If you have a partner, make sure your partner gets as much of a chance to do childcare as you do, so they can develop their parenting skills and form a bond with your child that doesn't go through you. And then if you're feeling fried, you can ask your partner to wrangle the kids while you recharge. (If you're being proactive, you'll work it out so each of you gets alone time regularly, so neither of you gets to the fried point.)

And whether you have a partner or not, you should start building a support network of friends and neighbors you can ask for help sometimes. If they like you, they are probably willing to take your kids for a few hours while you go to an appointment or recharge. But they probably don't think to offer, so you don't know until you ask.

Parenting is long, hard, tiring, occasionally demoralizing work. You don't have to white-knuckle through it alone. Reach out, whether you need emotional support or the physical presence of someone else, and your friends will be there for you.

You don't have to do it alone. People will help.

18: You can (and should) say "no"

When they're really little, we're so afraid of harming their gentle spirits that it can be tempting not to say "no." Ever. Instead we redirect, or give two choices, or do something else that guides them into doing what we want them to do without having to say "no."

But being a parent is about teaching your child how to be a person in the world, and in order to have harmonious personal relationships and contribute to society, a person has to understand limits and boundaries and appropriate behavior. And the only way to learn boundaries and appropriate behavior is for loving adults to make and enforce age-appropriate boundaries from the time a child is tiny.

So it's ok to say "no" when it's not good for your child to do something. Or even when you simply don't want your child to do something. It's ok to wean, to limit cookies or screen time or jumping on the couch, to force them to write thank-you notes, to give up their seats for older people, to let you eat your meal in peace. You don't have to justify saying "no," either, although you'll do more teaching if you tell them why so they can start sorting out what is and isn't acceptable. Kids need boundaries. They'll push against them, for sure-- that's what growing and developing is for. But if you don't enforce any boundaries they won't have any to push against, and they won't develop the way you want them to.

So say "no" with love, and stay firm, and your kids will grow up with healthy senses of themselves in the world.

You can do it.

19: You can (and should) say "yes"

Boundaries are amazingly important. But so is having fun and being joyful with your kids. Say "yes" as often as you can.

Say "yes" to being silly, to ice cream for dinner, to dance-offs, to leaving the kids with a babysitter so you can go out with your friends. Say "yes" to going on day trips together, to finding fairy doors, to making play dough, to playing soccer in the yard in the summer and the basement in the winter. Say "yes" to putting your toes in the sand, to running through the sprinkler, to catching lightning bugs. Say "yes" to going out to run around, or to stay inside snuggled up on the couch watching movies all day.

Say "yes" to things that feed your spirit and nourish you, alone and with your kids.

You spend so much time making sure they have everything they need. Spend some time making sure you all do the things you want, too.

"Our lives shall not be sweated from birth until life closes;
Hearts starve as well as bodies; give us bread, but give us
roses!"

Bread and Roses, James Oppenheim

20: You're supposed to think your kid poops rainbows

I hear people apologizing for saying nice things about their kids all the time, and I don't get it. Why would you feel bad about thinking your kid is great? You're your kid's parent-- it's your job to think your kid poops rainbows.

If you don't, who will? Of course you don't always think they're amazing, or even like them in the moment, but for the most part you probably think they're delightful. And everyone deserves to be loved completely, even with their faults. If you don't think your kid is fanfreakingtastic, they'll have a much harder time later on in life accepting complete love from someone else. By being the president of your kid's fan club now, you set them up for happy relationships later.

Thinking your kids are great doesn't mean enabling them to run wild and be disrespectful of others. Obviously you're still enforcing boundaries and teaching them how to interact responsibly with others and the world. But all with love, and not holding back the sense of wonder that this amazing person is your kid! So enjoy every interesting, weird, funny, excellent, magical thing about your kid, and feel good about enjoying it.

Keep going!

21: Worry is normal

Worry is one of the jobs of parenting. Stuff that you never thought about for yourself--how often you poop, whether you should eat honey or not, how many inches you've grown in the last six months, whether your teacher likes you or not-- becomes of paramount importance when it's about your kid.

That's all normal. I think it's biologically wired--if early people didn't worry and keep their infants close, those infants would be stolen by dingoes. We're still human, so it's still hardcoded in us to keep kids close and to worry about them. Thinking through the possibilities and how we'd deal with them helps us with mental flexibility and keeps us prepared for the inevitable crisis situations.

If your worry becomes so big that it takes over other parts of your life, and prevents you from having other emotions about your child and the other things you do, that's a sign that your hormones are out of whack and you need help. Tell your partner or a friend and they'll help you tell your doctor, and your doctor will get it straightened out. Overwhelming worry is treatable.

But normal worry, worry that's just one occasional emotion mixed in with all the other emotions, is part of being a parent. As your kids get older and more competent your worries will grow with them. But you'll be able to meet each stage, prepared, because the time you spent worrying gave your brain the chance to make plans for dealing with new situations.

You are doing it.

22: Your kid can do it

My 9-year-old just told me he wished he had a cupcake. So we looked up a mug cake recipe on the internet, he wrote it down, and now he's making it all by himself.

A few weeks ago, my 12-year-old was complaining about something and it turned into a rant breakdown of the difference between personal and systematic racism.

Your kids are going to get there.

Every day, you're putting in all this really hard work. From the physical labor to the emotional work, from showing them how to tie their shoes to potty training them to helping them practice reading to talking about current events and helping them interpret the big themes. It feels endless, like you're throwing it all into a bottomless pit. But you aren't. It's all going into them, and even when you don't see it having any effect, it is. They'll flip it back to you when you least expect it. And you'll be amazed at how thoughtful and competent and fully-formed your rainbow-pooping kids are. If my kids can make mug cakes and understand sociological phenomena, your kids can do those things and other impressive things, too.

You matter. The things you do and say matter every day, all the time. And your kids are soaking those up, and when they're ready, they'll shoot it all back at you, with mastery and swagger, and you'll see what excellent people they are.

You're doing it right.

23: You're going to make different decisions from your friends

You don't have to jump off a bridge just because your friends do. And you don't have to stop yourself from jumping just because your friends are glued to the railing. You know what's best for your kids and your family, and that's what you should do.

There are stages in parenting in which making different decisions from your friends can make it hard to be around each other. In the beginning, everything seems high-stakes. So if you're struggling with a decision or with having to carry through the decision you made, it might be difficult for you to be around someone who's made a different decision because it's too raw. (This is why sometimes it's hard for moms who breastfeed and moms who formula feed to hang out when their kids are teeny--the decision [such as it is] can feel too raw for either and both of you.) But once the decision loses some of the emotional power, you can be around each other, living out your different choices, with no problems.

(This is why moms of 8-year-olds rarely know and certainly don't care how the other moms fed their kids when they were infants.)

It can also be hard to be around your friends and their kids if they make decisions about teaching boundaries and limits that are very different from your own and you feel like their children aren't behaving in a way that you can be relaxed about. As you tell your kids, different families have different rules. If you need to take a break from spending time with a family that stresses you out, just take a break. Try to spend time with your friend away from their children so you aren't bothered by the parenting differences.

All these decisions we make--pacifier or no, where our kids sleep, bedtimes, babysitters, schooling, technology use, discipline, expectations, friends, family time--are all so important to us at the time. But that doesn't mean that there are absolutes in all categories, or that the same things have the same results with all kids (even with kids in the same families). So it's good to observe what your friends are doing, but then assess what results you'll have with your own kids, and make your decision based on that instead of what "everyone else" does.

This is tricky, but you're doing it.

24: It all goes by so fast

Pardon the sentimentality of this chapter. My first baby is starting seventh grade tomorrow, and he still looks exactly the same as he did the day he came out of me. Still those adorable huge cheeks. Still those deep watchful eyes. Still the most perfect face I've ever seen.

I know the minutes were long when he was a baby, especially the minutes after 1 am when we were both awake instead of asleep and I was pretending not to resent all that sleep time I was missing. I don't really remember much of the bad times. (I don't remember many of the good times from his first few years, to be quite honest. Sleep deprivation is real.) All the old ladies told me, "The minutes are long but the years are short," and they weren't kidding.

Twelve years, just like that. He's a fully-formed human, with opinions and ideas and goals and dreams that have nothing to do with me. I bet the next twelve go by just as quickly.

Take pictures. Tell stories of what your kids do. Save mementos of things you do and things that happen. Because you may not remember, and the next thing you know they'll be hugging you at eye level and tying neckties and cracking really sophisticated jokes. And you won't be sad that they're grown up, but you may wish you still had the little version of them at the same time, too.

Courage.

25: Emotions matter

Sometimes it feels like parenting is all logistical. Washing things, bending over to pick things up, folding things, putting things back where they belong, stuffing things in a bag and carrying them with you, making your kids put things down, kindly requesting that your kids give things to you, buying more of the right kind of things to prevent you from needing to buy more things. It's exhausting.

In the middle of all that doing, don't forget about being and feeling. Emotions matter. Your emotions matter. It's ok to feel irked or gleeful or sad or smug or whatever you're feeling. Even if feeling what you're feeling doesn't change the course of your day. Even if you still have to deal with all those things and all those jobs. You still get to feel what you feel, and you can tell the people who love you, and they will support you in whatever you're feeling.

The more you accept your own feelings, the easier it will be to accept your kids' feelings. And kids have some deep, serious, big feelings. The only way they'll learn to manage those feelings so they can get through life as smoothly as possible is if you help them by accepting their feelings and helping them put them in context. It's ok to be super-angry about putting on your shoes, but you still have to put on your shoes. Both those things can exist at the same time. You can be happy to be with your friend but scared that your friend is going to want to touch your favorite toy. Learning to navigate through big feelings is important, and it only happens when feelings are accepted.

The more you stay in touch with your feelings and your kids' feelings, the better you'll all get at supporting each other. One of you can have a bad day and get comfort from the others, who can be having an even better day because they were able to support someone they love. It all gets better and better, even when you're not feeling so great.

Your feelings matter.

26: No one gets a vote unless they're there at 3 am

I've been saying this one for years, but no one else gets a vote on what you do with your kid unless they're going to be there to enforce it and deal with the consequences.

All those people who tell you how to get your kid to sleep? If they're not going to be there with you at 3 am, they don't have a say. All those people who tell you where you should send your kid to school? If they're not there to deal with the feelings and homework at 4 pm, they don't have a say. All those people who want you to do this, that, or the other thing? If they're not standing next to your child when it all has to happen, just say #nope.

You know what's best for your kid. You. Not some stranger in the supermarket, or some book author, or your mother-in-law, or me. You. And if you don't know what works now, you'll think analytically about what you already know about your kid, and you'll come up with some things to try until one of them works. Because you're the parent.

You are doing it.

27: Your method of valuation changes

Before you have kids, figuring out the value of something is very straightforward. It's worth time, or money, or enjoyment, or some combination of the three. You can simplify a lot of things by figuring out if doing something has value to you. If it does, do it. If it doesn't have value to you, don't.

But once you become a parent, the whole concept of value changes. You find yourself doing all kinds of things that wouldn't have been worth anything to you but are worth something for your child. Touching someone else's feces, waking up multiple times a night, looking for a lost pacifier in the pitch dark. Driving long distances, paying for private schools, spending time on projects you can't stand, endless rounds of "The Wheels On The Bus," chaperoning One Direction concerts. Listening to long, elaborate, narratively dubious dreams. Picking the spoon up off the floor again. Showing up at the rink for practice at 7 am on a Saturday. It's a seemingly endless list of things you would never in a million years have done for yourself, but now you do with joy. (A cranky joy, sure, but joy.)

Investors can calculate the Net Present Value--how much the total value of something that will happen in the future is worth to them now--of any potential business venture to decide if they should do it or not. If the Net Present Value (NPV), or how much something is worth from start to finish, is worth more than the cost of spending time doing that activity, then it's worth doing that activity. The NPV of activities for parents is simple: Does it have value to or for your child? If so, then the NPV is higher than the opportunity cost and you do it. Gladly.

You are making the right choices.

28: Parenting can cause trauma

Parenting involves a lot of low-level but constant trauma. Everything from the chronic sleep deprivation to the physical stress to the worry to the isolation. Unless you have a ton of support around you constantly, it's impossible to escape feeling isolated and stressed (either a little stressed or a lot stressed), pretty much constantly for the first few years of your kid's life. Add another few years for each kid. And some parents continue to feel a lot of stress for years and years, depending on their family set-up, finances, school situation, childcare situation, etc.

I believe that a lot of parents are carrying around some trauma from our children's younger years, and may still be immersed in that trauma.

No wonder we're tired, and carrying around some extra weight, not sleeping well, and feeling like there are days we just can't get it together. I don't know how we heal ourselves, but I believe that rest and physical movement and good food and tons of water are key. Along with as much laughter and loving contact as we can find. And a healthy dose of cutting ourselves an enormous break.

This is hard. We're not broken, but we're scarred. We can do it.

29: You are going to have to make some hard choices

Kids force you into making decisions you never thought you'd have to make, and give you a different set of priorities. The ideas you have about yourself and about what your life is going to look like change after you have kids, and as your kids get older. In things as simple as getting rid of your expensive super-awesome coffee table, to things as complicated as deciding to end relationships that don't nourish you or allow you to be the best parent you can be. From making decisions about the kind of music you listen to while your kids are around, to deciding to push harder into your career or pull back from your career.

It's a double consciousness. For those of us who feel joy and connection in parenting, it means being forced into decisions you didn't know you'd have to make. And for parents who aren't feeling like there's much happening except a lot of work, it can be disheartening to lose options by having to choose only things that benefit your kid. Even when you're absolutely sure of and satisfied with the decisions, you still wouldn't have been forced to make them in such a deliberate manner if not for your child. When you sign on to have a kid, you don't really realize that part of being a parent is looking at all the rest of your life through the lens of what's best for your kid.

Even if it's for the best, it's still the end of your own innocence. And that can be hard.

Courage.

30: You can (and should) be true to yourself

I think a lot of us come into parenting thinking we have to be perfect. Or at least different from who we are. A G-rated version of ourselves, or someone better than we actually are. Smoothed out. We're supposed to be super-patient, strongly-bonded, overflowing with milk and kisses, morally unassailable, fascinated by truly dreadful children's music, uninterested in anything that isn't purely enriching, without tattoos or scars or baggage, and simply delighted to do anything that causes joy in little hearts, no matter how boring, odious, anxiety-inducing, or sanitized it is.

Well, hell. That's just not true.

If kids needed a beatific, generic parent we'd hold auditions for a Ma Ingalls doppleganger and then send all of our children off to her to raise. Ma Ingalls was the perfect, personality-less parent, and she'd do things technically well but your kids would be miserable. Your kids need you. Not just in your role as parent, but for yourself. Little (and big) weirdnesses and all. I could launch into some big stories about how weird my parents are and how funny that is and how endearing. Or I could tell you about how my son was telling me genetics have nothing to do with personality and I looked at him and said, "YOU'RE EXACTLY LIKE ME" and he laughed because he knows it's true, even down to our stress behaviors. But you have those same stories about your parents and your kids are going to have those same stories about you.

You are great. And part of what makes you a good parent is that you're still yourself. You stand for something. You're interested in things. You're working through it. And all those thoughts and all that process helps you be a person your kids can depend on, to love them and to help guide them through the process of growing up and being a human. Not a cardboard perfect parent (who won't have any sympathy when they screw up). Your learning to be human helps them learn to be human.

Keep being you you you you you. (And if you've been afraid to be the real you around your kids, start. Slowly. But start.) Then your kids get the security of a real parent, and they get to love the real you, and you get to love them with your whole heart.

This is scary, deep work, and you are doing it.

31: It's a wonderful life

You knew I couldn't end on a painful note, and I'm not: With all its trials and exhaustion, parenting is still a transformative gig, your best chance to love someone without an agenda and to be loved for exactly who you are.

The minutes can be excruciatingly long, especially at 3 am. But when you look up and see your child's sweet cheek--baby-soft or teen-roughened--and you love your child the person, that's when it all comes together. You have done this, and you are doing this, and it is complicated and nuanced and chaotic and delicious.

Keep going.

About the Author

*"If you have come to help me, you are wasting your time;
but if you are here because your liberation is bound up with
mine, then let us work together." -- Lilla Watson*

I'm Magda Pecsenye and I write the parenting advice website
AskMoxie.org. My expertise is in helping people be who they
want to be, with a specialty in how being a parent fits into
everything else.

I like people. I like parents. I think you're doing a fantastic
job. The nitty-gritty of what you do with your kids is up to
you, although I'm happy to post questions on the website to
get data points of how you could try approaching different
stages, because, let's face it, this shit is hard.

As for me, I have two kids who sleep through the night and
can tie their own shoes. I've been a married SAHM, a
married freelance WAHM, a divorcing WOHM, a divorced
WOHM, and now a WAHM again. I'm not buying the
Mommy Wars and I'll come sit next to you no matter how
you're feeding your kid. When in doubt, follow the money
trail. And don't believe the hype.

I think you already have everything in you that you need or
will ever need to be a great parent. You're the best parent for
your child.

About AskMoxie.org

Parenting advice website AskMoxie.org began in November 2005 with a simple post about trusting your own instincts and being careful not to place your trust in experts. From that first post, the motto of the website was "You're the best parent for your child."

A cult favorite, AskMoxie.org has always had a loyal group of readers and commenters, who have supported each other and helped each other become better parents over the past nine years. It remains mostly fight-free and troll-free, a place where people can consider their decisions without having to take sides, and a place where people can be proud of learning and becoming the parents they want to be.

Made in the USA
Middletown, DE
29 December 2014